THE ART OF POSITIVE COMMUNICATION

A practitioner's guide to managing behaviour

Rob Long

David Fulton Publishers Ltd
The Chiswick Centre, 414 Chiswick High Road, London W4 5TF

www.fultonpublishers.co.uk

First published in Great Britain by David Fulton Publishers in association
with the National Association for Special Educational Needs (NASEN)

NASEN is a registered charity no. 1007023.

David Fulton Publishers is a division of Granada Learning Limited, part
of ITV plc.

British Library Cataloguing in Publication Data
A catalogue record for this book is available from the British Library.

ISBN 184312 367 3

Typeset by FiSH Books, London
Printed and bound in Great Britain

Contents

1 Introduction

What is 'communication'?

This is a simple question about a process that we use all the time and yet is rarely considered. In every school, in every classroom, it is communication that sets the tone of any interaction between an adult and a young person. The interaction can be warm, friendly and enjoyable or it may be soured with negativity and hostility. A well-turned phrase can make or break a student's day.

Communication is the process by which information ('the message') is sent from one person – the sender – to another – the receiver. Messages are made up of many components:

verbal
- words

nonverbal
- tone of voice
- facial expressions
- body stance
- gestures
- proximity.

It is through listening to the whole message, by paying attention to the nonverbal cues, that we are able to understand not only what is said but also the emotional state of the person. The way that we say 'It's good to see you', for example, carries more information than the words themselves. The tone of the speaker's voice, degree of eye contact and body posture will each affect the way in which the message is interpreted regarding the emotional state of the speaker. Listening is an active process but, because it takes place so quickly and subconsciously, we are – for most of the time – unaware of it.

1

We may speak with our voices but we communicate with our whole body. Everything that a sender says or does can be interpreted as part of the message, and up to 90% of the message is sent nonverbally.

The number of communications we make each day is phenomenal and, because they are so frequent and so natural, we rarely take the time to reflect on our particular style. This booklet will enable you to review key aspects of your own communication style as well as to consider some different techniques for handling those 'difficult situations' that all school staff meeting during the day. These include the times when students carry on talking while class instructions are being given, demand excessive attention or use inappropriate language.

Our students have a sense of how we feel about them from the way we talk to them. Young people are influenced by the way in which adults relate to them and positive relationships develop from positive communication skills. Schools encourage and support students in many ways – through the use of rewards and certificates, for example – but one of the most powerful, and sometimes least understood, forms of encouragement, is in the feedback adults give to students, which can affect their self-esteem.

Self-assessment

Before we go any further it might be helpful to take a snapshot of how you feel about your existing communication skills by completing the questionnaire on the following pages.

Do you communicate positively?

Circle Y (yes), N (no) or S (sometimes) in response to the following statements:

- I always listen to my students' points of view.   Y   N   S
- I smile and laugh with my students.   Y   N   S
- I ask misbehaving students what helped them last time the situation occurred.   Y   N   S

- My behaviour management approach is to 'catch them doing good'.

  Y N S
- I often leave a student with a choice and then withdraw. Y N S
- When giving instructions I say 'thank you' rather than 'please'. Y N S
- Initially I use the lightest intervention possible to correct behaviour.

  Y N S
- When correcting behaviour I avoid being distracted. I stay focused.

  Y N S
- If students are angry I raise my voice, but do not get angry myself.

  Y N S
- If a student is being disruptive I ask him/her to say which class rule is being broken. Y N S
- I criticise the behaviour that prevents the task at hand, not the person.

  Y N S
- I encourage students to recognise and value their efforts and progress.

  Y N S
- I make a point of hearing the students' issues when problems occur.

  Y N S
- When possible I help students understand the emotions they are feeling and why. Y N S
- I remind misbehaving students of the consequences of their behaviour.

  Y N S
- To improve behaviour I ask students what it is that they should be doing.

  Y N S
- I make sure students know that I am looking out for improvements.

  Y N S

- I assure students that working together we can find a better way forward. Y N S
- I often remind students of previous agreements, such as to ask for help from the teaching assistant. Y N S
- I use a wide and varied range of positive verbal descriptions of behaviour, such as 'clever', 'imaginative', 'interesting', 'creative', etc. Y N S

Your score

Yes _____   No _____   Sometimes _____

Interpretation of your score

Note that different questions in the above list focus on different communication skills, which you should be aware of when checking your score:

- language and listening skills: nos. 1, 2, 6, 12, 14, 20
- solution-focused responses: nos. 3, 4, 10, 16, 17, 19
- reactions to misbehaviour: nos. 5, 7, 8, 9, 11, 13, 15, 18.

How many questions did you answer with a positive 'Yes'?

Above 15
You are already a skilled communicator.

Between 10 and 15
You are competent and aware of areas to develop.

Below 10
This booklet is the start of developing your communication skills.

HOT TIP Here and now

To enhance a positive sense of community use 'we' and 'our' rather than 'I' and 'my'. For example you might observe: 'This is one of the class rules that we all discussed and agreed on last week: that we would listen to other people's viewpoints without interrupting them.' Similarly a teacher might say, 'One of our golden rules is that we always put our hand up to answer questions.' Use students' names often. Give immediate nonverbal feedback – smiling, positive gestures, eye contact.

Whatever your score, being an effective communicator is a key skill that will benefit from having an 'MOT'. The fact is that we have each developed our own communication style that has been influenced by a range of factors such as:

- family experiences – how our parents praised and corrected our own behaviour
- temperament – some of us are naturally more volatile and easier to anger than others
- educational background – how we learnt to reflect about our own behaviour.

We each have a preferred way of relating to students in difficult and challenging situations. When students express needs that interfere either with others' learning, our teaching, or both, we react automatically according to our mental template.

Can you detect your communication style?

Without pausing to reflect, read the statements below and quickly confirm Yes or No.

Do you AVOID and try to withdraw?

- There are times when I let others take responsibility for solving the problem.   Y   N
- I try to do whatever it takes to avoid unnecessary tensions.   Y   N
- I sometimes avoid taking positions which would create controversy.
                                                                                                          Y   N
- If it makes other people happy, I might let them maintain their views.
                                                                                                          Y   N
- I feel that differences are not always worth worrying about.   Y   N
- I'd rather concede a point than have an argument.   Y   N

Do you ACCOMMODATE *and try to smooth out differences?*

- Rather than negotiate the things on which we disagree, I try to stress those things upon which we both agree.   Y   N
- I might try to soothe the other person's feelings and preserve our relationship.   Y   N
- I sometimes sacrifice my own wishes for the wishes of the other person.   Y   N
- I try not to hurt the other person's feelings.   Y   N
- If it makes other people happy, I might let them maintain their views.   Y   N
- In approaching negotiations, I try to be considerate of the other person's wishes.   Y   N

Do you COMPETE *and try to win at all costs?*

- I will never give in without a fight.   Y   N
- I try to win my position.   Y   N
- I am usually firm in pursuing my goals.   Y   N
- I make some effort to get my way.   Y   N
- I press to get my points made.   Y   N
- I assert my wishes.   Y   N

Do you COLLABORATE *and try to problem-solve?*

- I attempt to deal with all of the other person's concerns and my own.   Y   N
- I consistently seek the other person's help in working out a solution.   Y   N
- I always share the problem with the other person so that we can work it out.   Y   N
- I attempt immediately to work through our differences.   Y   N
- I always lean toward a direct discussion of the problem.   Y   N
- In approaching negotiations I try to be considerate of the other person's wishes.   Y   N

Do you COMPROMISE and ensure that there is a 'win–win' outcome?

- I try to find a compromise solution.   Y   N
- I give up some points in exchange for others.   Y   N
- I will let the other person have some of his/her positions if s/he
  lets me have some of mine.   Y   N
- I try to find a fair combination of gains and losses for both of us. Y   N
- I propose a middle ground.   Y   N
- I am nearly always concerned with satisfying all our wishes.   Y   N

Interpretation of your answers

Place your yes score in the radar graph below to discover your communication style. No style is in itself right or wrong – the problem arises when we over-use one style irrespective of the circumstances. High 'yes' scores in any style may reflect an over-reliance on that style. The ability to be flexible is a strength. You may well find that you have an even profile – which is normal. Specific troughs highlight areas to develop.

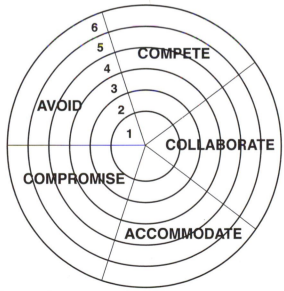

FIGURE 1. Radar graph

2 Forming relationships: accentuate the positive

It is strange that the one subject that we all experience and value is the one thing we receive the least training in: relationships. It is relationships that give our lives meaning yet they are the one thing that we receive little help with – until they go wrong.

We each experience relationships through our own frame of reference, which is part of our cultural identity. We select, organise and interpret our world through the influence of our culture and, without being directly conscious of it, our values and beliefs shape the meaning we find in any relationship. It is important to appreciate that it is for this reason that no two people experience any interaction in exactly the same way. It also follows that, if our values and beliefs differ greatly from another person's, then it can prevent us from understanding their method of communication. This explains why we find some students easier to relate to than others. As professionals we need to be aware of and actively explore the cultural frame of reference through which our students view the learning context.

Listening

True communication involves listening as well as talking. (It is interesting that we have two ears and only one mouth.) Too often we concentrate on the sending side of the communication equation, not the listening side, because most of us think we are naturally good listeners. Real listening is called 'active listening' and, when working with young people, it is as fundamental as sending the message. Listening enhances rapport in a relationship because it shows that you are concerned and wish to understand what is being said.

Paradoxical instruction

If a difficult and defiant student decides to walk away from you say to them, 'That's OK. You go for a walk and we will talk about this later.' The student is now not defying you but instead carrying out your instructions and not being defiant.

Three main barriers to listening

Response rehearsal
We are too busy rehearsing in our head what we are going to say when the other person stops speaking because, for example, we want to tell them something interesting that happened to us yesterday.

Preoccupied
When we have personal worries these can drain our energy and stop us from concentrating on what is being said. We will find that our mind keeps returning to our own concern (such as our overdraft) rather than truly listening to the other person.

Stimulus reactions
Certain words or phrases can have such strong emotional associations for us that when we hear them we are immediately distracted from hearing the message being sent. For example, someone says the word 'audit' and we are reminded that in four week's time Ofsted are coming and we are not ready.

Active listening

Good listening involves attending to many messages at the same time and being able to select and respond to those most relevant. There is a lot of 'noise' in any communication – that is, irrelevant and distracting information. As a result we do not always correctly receive and interpret the message that is being sent. 'You told me that you were really happy in school. But the way you said it, the tone of your voice and your body posture, made me think that you were anything but happy.'

The main difference between everyday listening and active listening is that in active listening the listener makes every effort to check that he or she really understands what is being said as well as helping the speaker understand it him/herself. Before moving on to consider how we send messages we need to highlight some of the key skills of effective listening. Some you will recognise as already being part of your repertoire; others might be new and need practising.

Key skills of effective listening

Encouraging

The right sort of encouragement enables a student to feel safe enough to make a contribution. Young people are often more used to being told what they should think or do, or questioned about their behaviour. Open-ended questions can lend support to the feeling that the listener genuinely wants to hear their views. Examples might be:

- 'You are doing a really good job. What are you planning to do next?'
- 'Look how much better you are getting on now. What skills have you used to achieve this?'

Paraphrasing

By paraphrasing what the student has said you show understanding of the message that he or she has 'sent'. For example you might say:

- 'Let's see if I've got this right. You're saying that you are less anxious during playtimes than you were last week?'

HOT TIP **Secondary behaviours**

Students can be very clever at distracting adults from their focus. Secondary behaviours such as looking away, the sneer, the mumbled comment can all result in the adult switching his/her attention from the target concern to another concern – which is of the student's making. Stay focused: 'We need to talk about your lack of homework. If we can't do so now I will see you later.'

- 'So what we have talked about so far is this. You have changed your route home and always wait for your two friends.'

Summarising

By summarising what the young person has said you show understanding of the main points contained within several messages, for example:

- 'To sum it up, then. What you are saying is that when you sit at the front of the class you can hear other children calling you names and it is making you very tense and frightened. Would you agree with that?'

Clarifying

This is necessary to establish meaning when the message is confused or uncertain, such as:

- 'What do you mean when you say you feel put upon?'
- 'Can I just see if I have got this right? When the instructions are written down for you, you don't have to worry about remembering them?'
- 'I am not sure if I understand you. Could you tell me a bit more? If I was in the playground with you, what would I see happening?'

Empathising

Empathising with the young person shows them your appreciation of their feelings. You might say:

- 'I understand how having someone push in front of you made you feel very angry.'
- 'I know you are feeling sad that your best friend is moving away.'
- 'With all the work you have to do to catch up it's not surprising that you feel worried.'

HOT TIP Visual displays

Display your Class Rules visually. When a rule is broken, point to the relevant part and just say 'Rule 3'.

Probing
Sometimes it is necessary to probe in order to obtain more information about a subject that the young person has introduced but not fully explained. You might ask, for example:

- 'Can you tell me more about what Sam was doing to stop you working?'
- 'Can you think of an example of the games that you feel unhappy about joining in with?'

Challenging
You may need to challenge young people when their ideas and/or actions seem to conflict, for example:

- 'Isn't this different to what you were just telling me? You said one of your best friends was Joanna.'
- 'I'm confused. On the one hand you seem to be saying that you enjoy your time out of class for extra help, but now you're telling me that you are being made to feel different from the rest of the class.'

Linking
This helps the student to reflect on ideas that appear to relate, such as:

- 'Earlier you said you really enjoyed PE – football especially – and now you're saying you wish you had some out-of-school interests.'
- 'Can you see any similarities between what you are saying now about how much you enjoy listening to music and what you said earlier about being unsure of which subjects to take next year?'

Descriptive observation
This helps the young person to find possible meanings to what they have said or done? This might be by saying, for example:

- 'You said you were happy that you had a change of teacher, but you sounded so sad.'
- 'Do you notice that whenever you mention William, you smile?'

Ask good questions

Asking 'why?' questions usually leads to a defensive response. Instead ask 'what?' or 'how?' A good question is, 'What would you like to have happen?' It encourages the student to focus on a positive goal.

When you start to listen actively don't be surprised that you keep making such mistakes as:

- interrupting
- asking too many questions
- offering solutions.

Whenever we try to break old habits relapse is normal. The more you practise, however, the quicker you will establish new habits.

3 Nonverbal behaviour

It is so easy in a learning context to take an over-rational view of both ourselves and our students. We forget – at our peril – the fact that we each have cultural and biological templates through which all information is perceived. These lead us to obtain much more information, albeit subconsciously, from nonverbal cues than from verbal ones. Our brain, for example, is pre-programmed with 'fight or flight' responses to danger. As a result a finger being waved in our face might cause a stronger reaction than might be expected. Similarly, as a culture we tend to stand at a certain, acceptable distance from each other. If someone enters our 'personal space' we can feel threatened.

When you ask a friend, 'How are you?' and they reply, 'I'm fine', you might respond, 'What's wrong?' because you have detected in their intonation a clear sign of unhappiness. This confirms the adage, 'It ain't what you say, it's the way that you say it.'

Following from this, within the classroom the way we convey information nonverbally can have a huge impact on our relationship with our students. Below is a list of those areas to be aware of, as well as ideas as to how we can convey our respect and value for our students without even thinking about the content of what we are saying.

HOT TIP Selective listening

Remember, many students will be looking for your buttons – those things that you overreact to. Practise ignoring minor behaviour disturbances – stay with the positive.

The power of silence

After you give an instruction to a student take two deep breaths and pause while you wait for compliance. Say no more than is absolutely necessary.

The term 'nonverbal behaviour' covers:

- facial expressions
- voice intonation
- gestures and postures.

Through nonverbal behaviours we can convey:

- interest vs. boredom
- affection vs. hostility
- concern vs. disregard.

As emotional beings, it is what is not said that conveys the messages we most wish to hear. Do you like me? Are you interested in me? Will you help me if I get stuck?

Nonverbal behaviour can be either positive or negative:

Positive nonverbal behaviours
- smiling
- eye contact
- meeting and greeting
- thanking
- avoiding intensive eye contact
- having your hands visual and open
- not entering students' personal space
- avoiding finger pointing
- showing concern
- not being over-calm.

Negative nonverbal behaviours
- pointing can be interpreted as threat
- talking to the board shows more interest in the content than in the students
- invading a student's personal space with intense eye contact can trigger negative reactions
- shouting – your normal voice shows you are in control – the louder the voice the more the message is one of 'losing control'
- folding arms conveys a stand-offish attitude.

De-escalating conflict through nonverbal behaviours

When we are trying to impress or develop a friendship we subconsciously reflect the behaviour of the person we are interacting with. This is known as 'mirroring'. What is going on is a conversation between two people at a subconscious level. We take up a not dissimilar body posture and we modify how close we stand to each other so that we both feel comfortable. We develop an appropriate amount of eye contact and we 'take turns' in our conversations. A relationship develops through each of us subtly influencing the other's behaviours. When these processes do not take place normal relationships do not flourish.

Within a working relationship there is, then, a sense of reciprocity: 'You can influence me and I can influence you.'

HOT TIP Put the behaviour on the chair

When you challenge their behaviour students can easily believe that you don't like them. We understand the 'condemn the act not the child' motto, but it is not that easy for a young person. Write the behaviours that you are concerned about on a list and place the list on a chair. Explain to the student that it is these behaviours that you have a problem with, not them. You wish to work with them to improve these behaviours.

Small problems need small tools

Use the lightest touch to manage behaviour – avoid overreacting. There is no need to 'use a sledgehammer to crack a nut'.

The reason why young people so often have major confrontations with adults they do not know is that there is no history between them of one affecting the other's behaviour. Without that they can both become locked into an escalating spiral of confrontation – with neither being able to reduce the conflict. This is why *all* students are more positively manageable when we have established a relationship with them. As professionals, the more we can understand the nature of these 'off-stage' subconscious and nonverbal conversations the more we can constructively use them. We can ensure that the messages we are sending out are the ones we wish our students to receive, for example that we are firm and confident rather than aggressive and threatening.

When a student is agitated and becoming angry we can use nonverbal signals to help return them to a more normal state. Simply telling them to calm down can add fuel to an already inflamed situation, and any level of arousal in our own voice shows the student that his/her emotional state has affected ours. We need to modify our own behaviour to send out calming messages in an attempt to reduce the student's level of arousal, with calmer hand gestures, less threatening body language and non-confrontational words. Our knowledge of body language gives us a set of skills to manage individuals and groups of students. Without this it would be as though we were driving in a foreign country without a road map.

An old teachers' saying about students goes: 'They don't care how much you know until they know how much you care.' As you convey your respect and care for students you are investing in the emotional bank. If at a later time you need students to comply with a request they are more likely to, and if you make mistakes they are more likely to forgive you. It is worth paying attention to the messages you are conveying with your nonverbal behaviour in order to deter unnecessary power struggles.

4 Eliminate the negative

Messages and feelings

We all have ways of communicating with our students that we have
learned from our own past experiences. Some of these are less effective
than others – in fact, they can make difficult matters worse.

What happens is that we can be saying one thing but our nonverbal
messages can be contradicting the verbal content. The nonverbal part of
the message – communicated through tone of voice, body posture, facial
expressions, eye contact, proximity and use of silence, are interpreted
subconsciously – and affect the way the total message is received.

In the classroom an adult can convey his/her sense of uncertainty through
such behaviours as pacing, fidgeting, self-grooming, etc. All of these will
correctly be seen by students as signs of insecurity. This contrasts with
the adult who has a more relaxed but controlled posture – in-control
teachers will often lean casually on furniture.

Some ineffective communication ploys

Some examples of negative ways of addressing students are given below.
No doubt you can add to this list.

> **HOT TIP** Let's rewind
>
> When a student says or does something inappropriate don't react
> immediately. Give them an opportunity to change it. Say, 'I don't think
> that worked as well as it could have. Let's rewind it and see if we can
> do it better.' This can save a lot of minor problems unnecessarily
> escalating.

Sarcasm

- 'You knew you had a test today but you still managed to leave your book at home. That was pretty smart! We await your results with interest.'
- 'Is this your homework? I will have to take up Chinese to be able to read it.'

Threats

- 'Touch that switch once more and you'll be in detention.'
- 'If you don't spit that gum out this minute, I'm going to send you out of my lesson.'

Commands

- 'Clean up this room right now. I will not take no for an answer.'
- 'Help me carry these boxes in. Hurry up!'

Prophecy

- 'You lied to me about your homework, didn't you? Do you know what kind of person you are going to be when you grow up? A person nobody can trust, and nobody will like.'
- 'Just keep going on being selfish. You'll see, no one is ever going to want to be friends with you. They'll treat you as badly as you're treating people now. Then we'll see how you like it.'

Lecturing and moralising

- 'Do you think that was a nice thing to do – to grab that book from your friend? I can see you don't realise how important good manners are. What you have to understand is that if we expect people to be polite to us, then we must be polite to them in return. You wouldn't want anyone to grab things from you, would you? Then you shouldn't grab from anyone else. We do unto others as we would have others do unto us.'

It is so easy to produce in students the very opposite feelings from those we intend to. When students are disciplined in such ways there are basically one of two responses open to them.

HOT TIP
HOT TIP The Columbo strategy

Like the TV detective Columbo, be prepared to ask for the student's assistance: 'I've never worked with a student like you before. You've had lots of people try to help you. What would you try if you were in my shoes?'

Fight vs. flight

These biologically programmed responses result in either offensive behaviour – 'acting out' – or defensive behaviour – 'acting in'. Neither is good for learning. The characteristics of each are as follows:

Acting out
- verbally abusive
- disruptive
- threatening and challenging
- defiant
- angry.

Acting in
- passive withdrawal
- lack of initiative
- dependency on others
- self-blame
- guilt.

Confrontational and challenging communications will typically increase both offensive and defensive behaviour. Instead, by the use of positive communication techniques students who demonstrate either of these categories of behaviour can be managed in a positive and non-confrontational way. Different techniques are presented here for managing the two types of behaviour, but are not exclusive to each.

Techniques for managing students who are acting out

- Make sure the student is alert and attending to you before you attempt to talk to him/her. Use the student's name and make brief eye contact.
- Ask positive questions, such as 'Can you remember what you did last time that helped sort out this argument about using the computer?' Make sure your questions are constructive, that is, 'What should you be doing?' rather than, 'What are you doing?'
- Indicate consequences. Point out the problem behaviour and the consequences of it, for example, 'If you persist with shouting out you will have to stay behind to discuss the rule about how to get attention in my class in detail.' Instead of whining, 'Why can't you line up nicely?' say, 'Until there is no pushing and pulling we will not be able to go in for dinner.'
- Offer choices, such as, 'You have two choices. You can either return to your maths work or you can have five minutes to finish off your art work. I will come back shortly to see which you have chosen.'
- Demonstrate positive expectations of students: 'Now please put all the equipment away so that we are ready to begin the next task,' or, 'You need to put a lot more effort into your work to achieve the grade you are capable of.' Instead of highlighting negative behaviour – 'You are still fooling around' – tell them what you are looking for – 'I expect you to be settled and working on your next target.'
- Make it short and snappy. If a student is not wearing their jacket, instead of a long explanation, just say 'jacket'. If they are eating inappropriately, 'bin'.
- Focus on behaviour. Make clear to students that it is their behaviour that is the problem, not them. Write the problem behaviour down and place it on a seat – this helps them to focus on the problem as something separate from themselves. Explain to the student that you want to work with them to help them to manage the behaviour better.
- Be solution-focused. Instead of analysing the problem help the student understand what the conditions are that enable them to behave appropriately. For example, instead of trying to understand the explanation as to why the student had a fight during lunchtime yesterday,

| HOT TIP | **Something special** |

> **HOT TIP** **Something special**
> Find out what a student's special interest is. Then, for example, one day bring them a relevant magazine and say to them, 'I saw this in the market and couldn't help but think that you would be interested in it.'

try to help him/her explain why s/he did not get into a fight today. What was happening that prevented it? Who was the student with? What were they doing?

- Sensitively inject humour into the situation as a distracting technique. If a student is drawing cartoons instead of reading the set task, say, 'If we go on losing time like this I'll be retired before we find a solution to the science problem.'

- Side-step confrontations. Be prepared to withdraw from a confrontation, for example when a student claims they have not had their work back, by saying, 'We need to have a chat about this at the end of the lesson.'

- Provide distractions. Prepare a range of activities such as an ongoing project, a physical task of sorting equipment out or a message that needs to be taken somewhere. You can divert a student's attention with this when they are finding a certain task challenging.

- Show faith: say 'when' not 'if'. 'When' shows a definite expectation that the student will succeed, whereas 'if' shows doubt. For example, 'When you have finished that piece of work you can have ten minutes on the computer,' rather than, 'You can go on the computer if you finish the work.'

- 'Follow instructions with a 'thank you' rather than a 'please'. 'Thank you' shows an assumption that your instructions will be carried out: 'Back in the queue, thank you.'

Techniques for managing students who are acting in

- Skill development. Find out about students' interests and support them in enhancing and strengthening their skills through providing safe opportunities. If they are interested in cooking, for example, this can be used as some part of a project.

- Build self-esteem. Students will often feel negative towards themselves through seeing others who are more able and confident. Develop a daily programme to help raise their self-esteem. This would include relaxation activities, target-setting for success, time with friends, humour through watching favourite TV programmes, good self-care habits (such as diet and exercise).
- Send a student a note highlighting a success or thanking them for their help in some area. Many students rarely receive unsolicited appreciation from adults.
- Thought-stopping: teach the student to change their thinking. Help them to re-establish some positive memories and encourage them to practise thinking of them when they are feeling negative. An elastic band on the wrist can be pulled to help them snap out of the negative. The sudden snap can trigger them to stop the negative thinking and do something different.
- Target-setting. Succeeding at challenging but achievable targets will help to encourage students' positive views of themselves – providing they accept that it is their effort, not luck, that produced the result.
- Personalise feedback. Use a special term or name; for example if I only ever say 'you are my top scientific wizard' to one pupil it will have more impact. If you call everybody 'a star' then being a star is not special.
- Worry time. When students face issues that cannot be readily resolved teach them to have a short worry period – five minutes – after which they must get back on task. If the worrying thoughts try to creep in before the allotted time they must tell them to wait.
- Positive thinking. Spend time with students to help them appreciate the skills they have mastered over the years. Reinforce the notion that it was practice and determination that led to their success. Also encourage them to see many of their personal qualities as attributes that others like in them. Often what we see in ourselves as a vice our friends can see as a positive and enduring virtue.
- Story-telling. To help a student confront unpleasant situations and fears find relevant stories that explore similar issues in a positive way. For a student who is being bullied, for example, a story or TV soap that deals sensitively with this topic could be a useful learning and talking point. We all find it easier to confront our fears one remove

from ourselves – the emotional arousal is less, enabling us to consider the strategies that are used in the story.

- Relaxation. Exercises to relax muscles through tensing then relaxing, combined with breathing techniques (breathe in through the nose to the count of seven and out through the mouth to the count of ten), will help those students who are prone to anxiety. Once these skills are taught students can practise them anywhere and at any time.
- Catch them being good, for example, 'I really liked your contribution in the history lesson yesterday.' Be solution-focused instead of always analysing the difficulties: 'What do you think helped you to work so well for the last half of my lesson?' Find the 'exceptions' to any problem, that is when the problem is not as bad as usual: 'I noticed that you left your seat less than you usually do. Why do you think that was?' When things have gone well, help the student understand those factors that enabled that to happen. Such knowledge can be used to make these exceptions happen more often.
- Assertiveness training. From an understanding of their rights, as well as the rights of others, students can learn how to express themselves, manage confrontations and negotiate as well as how to accept criticism and receive compliments.
- Anchoring and mood-changing. A student can learn to trigger positive emotions through taking a strong, positive memory and exploring it in the fullest detail. Where are they? What are they wearing? Who are they with? What are the positive feelings they have inside? Now teach a basic behavioural cue – crossing two fingers. The student practises crossing fingers and re-experiencing the emotions associated with the memory. At times of negativity the trigger – crossing fingers – can pull out the positive feelings.

HOT TIP **What's in it for me?**

Before helping students develop an action plan, improve their determination to change by helping them see the gains of what is 'in it for them'.

- Problem-solving. Negative feelings usually tell us that things are not right for us. Teach the students how to explore a problem, generate possible solutions, choose one of those solutions to tackle the problem with, and afterwards to evaluate outcome. If, for example, the student is shy help them to explore ways of relaxing. Talk to them about those situations that they can manage and help them practise taking control of their feelings. Problems can be reframed as opportunities to improve these essential skills.

Some of the ideas in the above two lists are clearly applicable both to students who 'act out' and those who 'act in'. Never let an imposed classification system stop you using common sense – go with whatever technique helps an individual student.

Conclusion

To conclude then, good communication skills are the strongest tool that school staff have. Our voices are always with us. The tips and techniques detailed in this booklet will be familiar to many staff, and will encourage new staff to look carefully at their communication style. Positive communication is an effective way to manage young people's behaviour: it minimises stress and is successful and enjoyable.

Recommended reading

Bocchino, R. (1999) *Emotional Literacy*. Thousand Oaks, California: Corwin Press.

Brophy, J. (1998) *Motivating students to learn*. Boston, Massachusetts: McGraw Hill.

Friend, M. and Cook, L. (2000) *Interactions*. New York: Addison Wesley Longman.

Neall, L. (2002) *Bringing the best out of boys*. Stroud: Hawthorn Press.

Partin, R. (1999) *Classroom Teacher's Survival Guide*. West Nyack, New York: The Centre for Applied Research in Education.

Mackenzie, R. (1996) *Setting Limits in the Classroom*. Roseville, California: Prima Publishing.

Weare, K. (2000) *Promoting Mental and Social Health*. London: Routledge.

The complete set of titles in Rob Long's Building Success Through Better Behaviour series:

The Art of Positive Communication: A practitioner's guide to managing behaviour
1 84312 367 3

Better Behaviour
1 84312 363 0

Children's Thoughts and Feelings
1 84312 368 1

Loss and Separation
1 84312 364 9

Motivation
1 84312 365 7

Obsessive Compulsive Disorders
1 84312 366 5

Working with Groups
1 84312 371 1

Yeah Right! Adolescents in the classroom
1 84312 370 3

David Fulton Publishers

Special Needs and Drug Education	1-84312-360-6	£12.00
Supporting Mathematical Thinking	1-84312-362-2	£18.00
Dyslexia and Inclusion	1-84312-361-4	£17.00

To order these books please contact:
David Fulton Publishers Ltd
The Chiswick Centre • 414 Chiswick High Road • London W4 5TF
Tel: 020 8996 3610 • Fax: 020 8996 3622
www.fultonpublishers.co.uk